SEVEN NOTES OF A DEAD MAN'S SONG

Bernd Sauermann

MadHat Press
Asheville, North Carolina

MadHat Press
MadHat Incorporated
PO Box 8364, Asheville, NC 28814

The Library of Congress has assigned
this edition a Control Number of
2014915660

ISBN 978-1-941196-06-9 (paperback)

Text by Bernd Sauermann
Cover photograph by Marc Vincenz
Book and cover design by MadHat Press

www.MadHat-Press.com

First Printing

SEVEN NOTES OF A DEAD MAN'S SONG

CONTENTS

FOREWORD

I have admired Bernd Sauermann's mysterious poems for decades. They are not approachable in the way that many, possibly most, poems are. Sauermann asks for a leap of faith from his readers, a leap which is quickly earned through the sheer brilliance of his language: "And then years push between us like a throbbing tooth." "My ears burn with starlight." "We mouth the equations of clouds whose shadows drift slowly across our root-bound hearts." "Explain to me again why we subject ourselves to the scrutiny of snow." "Two figures stand off in the distance. One is indifference and the other is regret." "Another curtain parts, slowly revealing a curtain." Out of the strangeness of Sauermann's language, even from these random haunting lines I have quoted, meaning does coalesce. I cannot say I understand how he makes it happen, but he does, and it is deeply affecting and often moving. Sauermann works in the prose poem, a form that easily takes shape in French but seldom seems to within the stresses of English. Yet in Bernd Sauermann's poignant voice, I hear the music and poetry I never seem to hear from other prose poets. But perhaps it is because, as he says, he "play[s] the cast iron flutes of the mythic." That, I think, is the unique, unfamiliar, yet beautiful sound I have always heard in his work.

— John Wood

For Amanda

Is death so strong a word now
That over the earth life shall not be worshipped
in the clarity of steel?

--MacKnight Black, Machinery

OBSERVATOR

LIGHT YEARS

The song, the murmur, the pleasure of tresses, the spent buds on the trees raining on us like whispered yes's. The rush of touches being committed to memory. This distance seems so hard on a gray morning with the window open like a mouth and all this wind listening like soft breathing. Memory of a shiver, a titter of a breeze and the cool night at the foot of a mountain. This distance seems so hard on any given day, the here and now delicate as a window, imperceptible as the mountain off over there somewhere in the night. I train my ears for a forgiving phrase, recall that the color of an eye is still etched in stained blue glass, though these billion light-years distant.

SIMILE

Accusations then and there and the right stays right even in and out of the bed we made these decades ago. Why does a forgotten word change its clothes so easily when the wind picks up? Isn't this a gathering of clouds? Aren't these slippery tongues? At the slick portal of a sentence, who doesn't harbor some small fear? Perhaps that a minute has ceased to pass, for instance, like a scar.

PLAN

Duration of a pleasure, the faint halo and the phase of a waning moon. Let's shy away from shadows and the stern gaze of mothers and fathers. Let's toss no murmured word into the road on any given night. Look into the light of shameless diction and the stars hide behind the safe curtains of clouds. I give you luggage; you give me transport to a neighboring town in which a small scent huddles in a trembling room. No door is locked forever. No window barred from ruthless love.

MARITIME

A flash of thigh is married to a short film about treason on the high seas as something sounds in the blackening deep. Something like a dolphin chitters. A phrase is happy in the sharpest mouth. Back at the boat, questions remained unasked as if language had not been invented. A reclining on the shore of a body of warm water. The scent of moisture in the air, and on the beach, a wave rolling like the turn of a slender hip. The change of tides seemed destined never to occur. The moon silently answered. We held still for what seemed like hours.

DARK MATTER

On a hillside in the cool leaves of the first fall night. I remember ... I will never ... Right now ... And then years push between us like a throbbing tooth. I remember clothes, a glance, perhaps an eyelash in a dimly lit stairwell. You remember tears falling like wet syllables. All the light that's ever washed over your streaked face now washes over mine and then buries itself deep in my palms. Galaxies keep spinning themselves out into the space between unbearable sighs. My ears burn with starlight.

Bernd Sauermann

THE NEW MATH

The pilloried median daffodil, derivative of a mean rose, the average petunia, the modal snapdragon. Every flower is new and forever and ever bathed in the glow of a gentle mathematics. And so the rain keeps falling somewhere in a parallel green universe where flags slap in a floral wind and flowers bloom like theorems planted in straight boy/girl boy/girl lines. We mouth the equations of clouds whose shadows drift slowly across our root-bound hearts.

NOCTURNE

Through listening to the stars. When scenting the night flowers. The deepening cobalt dusk. Somewhere off years ago a window is barred against intruders. We live our entire lives in fear of locks. So then, abandon is felt in two dimensions and a backward glance reveals two small breasts you had the audacity to show me in light of a hanged moon. Who are you now? Will you open the window? Will you take the night into your locked chest?

Maritime II

The beach of the lovely raft forgotten. Strong swimmer on a day of meager sun and breezes. Wet sand, the undertow. A lock of hair no longer exists, wet and clinging to the nape of a slender neck. Ten, twenty, thirty years from then, I breathe a molecule of air you once left at my feet. A grain of sand blown from the cup of an imagined palm confirms my fears as an hourglass shatters in my hand and makes me want to dig a hole, dig it deeper, and then climb in while the tide rises. This, despite anything I tell you about how tranquilized the sea is today.

METAMORPHIC

I mine your glance for anything of value. A world ends a hand's width away from the flicker of late-night TV as the notion of travel is discussed. Destinations are shuffled like a deck of face cards. We get in the car. When I roll down the window, it means that I need some air. When you roll down the window, it means that I will dance with a stranger at a bar in a city where I won't know you anymore. You will speak in the voice of a stranger and my heart will crack like granite to reveal a vein of dull, silent ore.

PORTENTS

Obsessions twist like weather, the cold receptacle of an upturned palm, the casual dismissal of everything near the familiar center. A temple of hands is built in the morning of blue light. There are footsteps in the snows of last night's passing, and soon, soon the footsteps will be black. Smoke, too, will rise like a threatening hand from somewhere off in the distance.

THE NATURE OF SCENT

The salt, a trace of all your tears, scattered to thaw the slivers of a thousand frozen days. Another tract of silent letters in the basement of averted eyes. Years later, learning how to get bigger mirrors the rising light, fills another minute, then another. Soon an event will surface like a bruise. Footsteps stop a hand from recalling the fond hours of darkness. A bed retains the scent of ink like a black sheet in the dim morning light, where formerly an arm shone.

ASTRONOMY 101

Perihelion, the last few hours of one more night, photons advancing, filling the black holes between our words. We knew that an ending had arrived when we watched the moon slump toward the horizon. There exists a star, dark matter, and there exists a body of light. A galaxy in someone else's eyes, the impersonal distance of ether.

INTERSECTION

Then the corner of triste and giddy, memories yet to commit, so much like a busy intersection after the cars have left. So lovely walks the sun, so careless, and the grass nodding in approval. Yet there stands an invisible tree so sad one can hear its muffled sobs. It's true; I can't afford one million sighs and no stars will fall into your hand or mine at this intersection of obligatory gestures made in some other universe.

LET'S GO

Fifteen minutes to sunshine, warmth, the breeze, the sidewalk. The going home, the lonely pleasure of a wanted dead or alive communiqué. I will break your heart like an ashtray since every day has arrived like one precise cloud in a broken sky. The short walk to the car, a phrase waiting in an open mouth, all revved up and ready to drive. Do you have a light? Hand me that ashtray. Hand me your mouth, so close to the whirring blades of the sky.

ONE REASON

Glass shatters like a window through which I see a woman undress. A woman is a bullet in the drawer of an outlaw. An outlaw is a drawn-out moan overheard in passing. A man leaves town for a reason.

HEAT WAVE

It is decidedly summer. A short stint in the arms of a shimmering girl as a midday sun smolders. Rocks white in the face of the heat stare on. Eyes risen while bright gestures sink out of sight in the blue water, I salute this daily like a burning flag.

STAIRS

The smell of damp leaves in the woods at night. I hear you whisper about a change of season approaching. Yes, I say, the season of leaving arrives. Soon, a stairwell will deliver me from a single phrase. Soon, a stairwell will reduce me to a point in time. Soon, a stairwell will no longer hiss its sad threat. But then morning will offer its soft apologies. A turning point approaches. Enough, you say, and kiss me.

Bernd Sauermann

An Allegory

In this country, there is a girl from the high-rise who is murdered. Surely, that same girl was not the one I kissed in the woods. This much I'm sure of, I tell all my friends; I loved her and she loved me for all of an afternoon. Later I'm told it was all a lie. There was no girl. There was no high-rise. There was no murder. This much I'm sure of, I tell all my friends; there was an afternoon in a country where I spoke the language in the manner of a native.

PHYSICS

Apples rot on the ground and smell like wine. A bus passes in the cold blue light of evening. On it, there are warm people going to warm places. They look warm. Someone sitting alone on a small hill notices this.

ENTRANCE

There is a field behind the girly bar. There is a girl in that field, and I am with her. Later, we explore a dark basement room. Years later I am that dark basement room itself. I open the door. I go in.

NOTHING

Anniversary of a day gone rarely bad. Annealed like metal in front of a crowd. The alarm takes us outside amidst the others who know nothing of ashes. A car parked beneath the high-rise remembers nothing. A sky rise remembers nothing. A party of fools under the spell of jazz remembers nothing. A red suede boot, a black skirt, and a strand of pearls--nothing. A scar across the bridge of a nose--nothing. It's nothing, I mutter, and become silent.

THAW

Years later, we walk slowly out to the point, its rocks dulling themselves against January ice. We sniffle stiff promises as our planned life careens like a distant galaxy. Then a lie breaks into someone's ear. We learn the hard way that love holds a silver bowl under our noses, that a blue coat equals what a hole is to sand. We learn that a stone thrown out on the ice waits until spring to sink.

INVISIBLE INK

Like wisps of mist skirting the summit of the knoll, seven deer drift through a meadow of skulls and then slowly disappear. I wake up and I scribble this down in vanishing ink, then drift back off into seven minutes of twitching sleep. In such a way this morning functions: window up, winter pallor, bracing gusts of wind, and every seven minutes the alarm breaking the grief heavy and gray as a dream. Then, slowly, everything becoming illegible again.

Bernd Sauermann

TRACKS

Our room is inhabited by the ghosts of winter. Outside a cold settles like snow into our boot prints. Tell me again why we have walked here. Explain to me again why we subject ourselves to the scrutiny of snow. Repeat the vows we have taken meaning to keep like plastic flowers. Tell me again why these woods feel so empty.

SOME QUESTIONS

The river tells us lies about the moon and wind, but I have no words to offer of my own. Two figures stand off in the distance. One is indifference and the other is regret. They chat uncomfortably about the phrases floating like sticks under the bridge. Soon, on a torrent, a paragraph spins like deceit. Why do things always come to this? The river answers this question with another. Whose language is this, anyway? Whose mouth?

Bernd Sauermann

A Scent Lingers

A cold wind shoulders the drapes. A fresh sheet of paper is slowly filled with someone else's words. The scent of paper on skin. The scent of ink on a woman's hands. What will the next day say about a poem written during a storm shattering the night like the flicker of late-night TV? Someone slowly approaches a door. A scent lingers.

THE END OF THE WORLD

When winds conspire on the knoll and the northern lights do their hushed shimmy. When no caps are worn backwards. When an arm glows warmly in the night. When no one hears what we are doing. When precautions have not been taken. When the world ends a hand's width away. When a silence shudders. When in the blue light of knowing. When after coffee. When after a silent house.

PARTING

Words all the time and a tricky walk down a rain-slick sidewalk; a man looking for a towel, hot lather, and a razor. He looks for hair at the temple, the faint hair on the nape of a neck, an angel's sweat on the head of pin. Every man is a failed saint, and every angel is a shock of damp hair on the bathroom floor. So the season of rain and bracing wind brings scissors, warm water, a window, slightly open. The season of leaving arrives. The curtains part slightly. They part wider.

DEAD MAN

No one is humming a dead man's tune. No one is waking a dead man up, and no one is selling a dead man's house. No one mutters the dead man's name and no one wears the mask that hid the dead man's fear: the fear of the woman in a wooden mood, the fear of the dead wind through the window, and the dead rain on the glass, the fear of the dead child in the closet. No one hears that the dead man's daughter talks too much, and no one sees the dead man's daughter one last time at the store, that the dead man's rearview mirror has no heart, that seven dead birds take to black flight like seven notes of a dead man's song.

Bernd Sauermann

IT TASTES LIKE SILENCE

How long has one word remained unsaid hunching in the tree line like a mute wolf? How long has a screen door ceased to swing on the slightest breeze? How long has this sentence been unhinged? I come to this not easily: there is weather and there are storms that topple oaks not hung with chains of unsaid rumors. I mouth the word. I try it out. I try it out and it tastes like silence. It tastes like the silence after the wolves stop howling.

THE CAUSE OF DEATH

When the old dream resurfaces like a cadaver, you will be my grappling hook to toss out over the thing, to pull it back for a trip to the morgue. The results of the autopsy go without saying. But where will I go when my energy dissipates? Where will I go when my eyes no longer look at the surface of things but drip from my skull like eggs ready for the skillet? Oh, if only to enjoy a breakfast of shrimp wrapped in bacon to be eaten in the light blue of a winter labeled 'winter,' to enjoy a cup of coffee labeled 'coffee,' a feast of nothing not labeled 'farewell.'

INTERFERENCE

Suddenly a new year has begun in a distant country. Surely there, the weather changes for the wetter. Surely moss drapes from the live oaks like wild hair. A fertile swamp breeds gestures free of miscommunicated intent. Uncertain words are sent over the wires. The words are received, barely heard like lies someone doesn't want to believe. It's not true, someone else says, adding yet another kink to the cable.

REVELATION

A new year brings rain to a distant state of mind. Finally, the weather has horribly broken. Finally, a curtain has parted to reveal a curtain. Night falls like ashes and I mean this in the best possible way. Looking out across the lake, invention attends the sunset. I have brought myself here for no-good reasons. A woman has a basket of food and wine. Slowly, she comes toward me. I offer her my dark balcony. I offer her my steep stairs. Slowly, she climbs them. Another curtain parts, slowly revealing a curtain.

CHEMISTRY

Skin denies me its surface, as a television crouches in the corner and tenses. The flowers are done blooming, but a continent away another seed is planted. The highway kills one half our teacher. Soon the television will get up and leave. Better living through chemicals.

THE VIEW FROM HERE

A dew rag and a dropped shot of gin. A dew rag and a late-night diner. A dew rag and a missed chance at sleep, a dream lopped off like a leg gone bad. The farther away from the castle the better. I call you there, tell you I am existing, here and now, in a moat.

LANGUAGE

In this way, not the distance, but days held down by time are spanned by waves of breath, grip of thumb and index finger, sweeping moves of hand, a pen, the begging white of empty paper. Erie to Lake Charles, like Earth to sun and back again, is distance only possible between her skin and mine, perfectly so out of touch. Glistening wind, let language assure proper direction and transport us steadily sunward so that we may burn.

CHEST

Possibility surfaces like an invented word. I am old; you are young. This is the yellow lie on the floor, the lie that was told with that knowing look and a skewed smile. There is chocolate on the pillow, and hope has turned back the covers and winks. Today, rich food will taste like doubloons and my chest will open like a trunk full of gold.

Exchange

Trees are swaying to the ebb and flow of time. In a small room in a basement, a rug is unrolled and a boy and girl get comfortable with each other. The room is filled with dark items. Soon, a lie will be born. The lie will be held briefly by the boy. Then, he will give it to the girl. This exchange of words will continue for days, weeks, years. Finally, the truth will emerge as a small bird. The truth will fly away as a small bird, and the truth will build a nest in the shape of a room. Isn't this the way it always ends? With words as fragile as small blue eggs?

AGAIN, APPLES

We explore any excuse for our inaction. In a small house the sound of a drawer opening is monumental. Later, we'll walk through an orchard on the way to where a boat is overturned in a garden. That night, we will sleep under that boat. Again, apples play a minor role in this. No hands clap to the sound of a distant woman, a woman far away who has not yet been committed to memory. And then, of course, there are the apples.

PINE

A woman walks slowly in the snow. A woman stoops under the downed pine and a fine powder drifts away like a distant future. Does a tree remember her secret name? Does a woman remember my hand, turned over and inspected and filled with dust? I see a forest and a face emerges. I see a tree and lips and nose and the memory of a scent returns like faint prints in a field of snow. Does the faint dream still exist? Has another wish fallen over? I am still not there for anyone to hear. A woman's name sounds like snow falling. The snow fills my nostrils with the silent scent of pine.

SLOW

Slow in the limbs, slow like Sunday's bells, like the motions of shaven angels. Slow like a stroll in the churchyard, a hand over a temple of stubble, the wind over a field, and slow like the tapestries of the cathedral. Slow like her thighs and slow like a room somber with smoke and candles. Slow like a hymn twisting itself to a breathless halt. Slow like the sober man sleeping on the floor amidst laundry. Then the quick scent of coffee and a shock of damp hair.

Bernd Sauermann

ALPHABET

An X appears on the head of a boy who will whisper. A Y appears on the head of a girl who will listen. This is the alphabet of heat. A word is formed on the tongue of the boy. That word is woven into the clear sentence of a summer day. I shout this out at the top of my lungs.

SOURCE OF MY MALADY

IRONCLAD

Say I obsess about the weather because I am a gunboat, which is to say I have firepower. Say there is a small craft advisory in effect in my chest. Say that I may light the fuse in my head and propel a thing in her direction. Say boom. There is a splintered tree floating down heart's river. There is a dinghy scuttled in the boathouse. Say the weather is filing a complaint about the continual reports.

MENU

Asking for trouble from the sleeping girl, you realize upon waking you are the proud owner of a restaurant, and in the thin light of morning, a breakfast seems as redundant as the thin light of morning. A cup labeled "cup" runneth over. A plate labeled "plate" assumes exciting positions while a dish labeled "memory" fades like the soft steam on the mirror. The spoon, the knife, and the cup of coffee dutifully follow. There is a fork in the road. There are bacon-wrapped scallops. There are, as they say, the shrimps. Good God, good morning, slightly saline light of day. All along and almost daily, it's been these hellish dawns. And then the heat, and finally, the required application of morning.

LESS IS MORE

Your lips shine more silent than the moon. Your lips dole out moisture like a drug, and your lips, like a slow summer shower, jettison all unneeded consonants. I am loath to stay within the defined area, soft and red as a mouth. Then your mouth fixates on my head an idea, a glistening notion, a sharp bartered haircut and a hint of dawn, breaking like a vowel. Then the necklace, a canvas, the broken leg of some stringed instrument. Then the face filmier than dust, the dust whiter and whiter than white. Then black. Then blacker. Then less than dust, less than anything.

Bernd Sauermann

WILD WEST DAZE

Wounded by the clouds, I am a pioneer, but a bandage of wind allows me to monitor healing. The way she fears horses suggests treatment has been received and working. So thanks for the glancing blow to the head. Thanks for the hair shirt. Thanks for stirrups, the saddle, and the scabbard. And thanks for this blanket of cast iron clouds and for this dank air slumping like wet wool. Evening clanks and these feelings bray like the morning on which hang all my equine fears—mine and mine and mine forever. Whinny. And you, you have discovered the source of my malady, a graceless notion of pain, its equestrian gesture made solely out of hair.

LAST CENTURY

Sweet eyes, a kind of flower comes to mind, and hair, all black but only at the ends. May I please speak to any woman named Ana? And as clouds move in and out and the sidewalk grows weary, I see boots in the corner of someone's mind, but they are slumped over like 1979. We tried very hard to not make noise that year. We took our shoes off at the door. I remember you kept saying something like a word, and I remember asking something like a question. The answer, a slurry yes yes yes. It began, after all, that darkest year, with no, then shone brighter in the middle, like maybe.

Bernd Sauermann

THE OLD SALOON BIT

Slap leather to the cadence of whorehouse sighs and the breathless slip of hips and thighs in a room above the saloon. In this town, the sheriff is always on duty. In this town, the hot pies cool safely on the old widow's window sill, and in this town there's always a dust storm on the horizon. But the barkeep polishing his tumblers seems not to notice. No one reaches for the sky, though the sheriff counts his bullets, being sure to push each one gently into the gleaming gun. This town is big enough for both of us, he thinks, but then she sashays down the stairs.

BANK ACCOUNT

Some days the words spew from my slot like coins. Say ingot. Say bars. Say jackpot and 24 carats. The gold wears gold to bed and drinks from golden cups. In this shining dream, I am paid to perform favors. This is the gold speaking, and If I don't get the gold, I didn't want it hard enough. This is the compounding of interest in the morning sun, when we can see the next few decades, our so-called golden years. I count on them. I hear the moaning of precious metal. I hear the chink of coins in the next century. Count me in and I will call us rich. I'm banking on this in my next life when you will be my safe deposit box and you will wear me like a heavy key around your neck.

Bernd Sauermann

DIESEL GENERATOR

I

I am aware of a slight tingling sensation, says the diesel generator. It emanates from under my scapula. No sooner has the diesel generator mouthed these words that a loud rumbling can be heard. The diesel generator does not look concerned because he is unflappable in his knowledge that might makes right. Just then, a door swings open and the diesel generator walks through. Another door opens and the diesel generator walks through. Through another door walks the diesel generator. This goes on for some time until the diesel generator signals enough. I notice the tingling sensation has now moved on down my arm, he says, toward my hand which holds tightly to this door knob.

Bernd Sauermann

II

I will shoot a hole through this Bible big enough to drive a goddamn truck through, says the diesel generator, and this lets me know that an impasse has been reached. Someone asks the diesel generator how he can be so sure of the existence of angels. I have seen them copulating on the head of a pin, he says, and just then, the diesel generator breaks into a slow dance much like clouds of blood in a hypodermic. I am showing you this dance to inform you of your transgression, he says, and then the diesel generator grins widely. In his mouth, a gun can be seen. A flash and a loud noise signal that the gun has been discharged as he turns the ignition of a large truck, but a cloud of diesel exhaust obscures what happens next.

III

The diesel generator is always writing something. I am writing about the advent of war, says the diesel generator. In this war, a man will come to discover that he is really a train. Across a bridge above the switching yard walks the diesel generator, and stops directly over a train. Looking down into the smokestack, the diesel generator thinks he has an idea. I think I'll write about this war in the first person, he says. And so begins the third installment in the acclaimed trilogy. I am a war, writes the diesel generator, and in me is a man who turns into a train.

IV

A hole signals the presence of nothing, thinks the diesel generator. Once, lying in a field with a girl, you had a similar thought. Here, said the girl, and offered her breasts. You were grateful, in retrospect, that the sky held no rain and that the grass was soft and cool. The girl nuzzled closer and expressed her love like warm milk. At her feet, a lake or a pond appeared in approval. Wavelets lapped at your toes. Surely there must be more to the story than that, suggests the diesel generator. Yes, you say, a hole opened in the sky and a blue light came pouring forth. A blue light, says the diesel generator, signals the presence of a lie. You think about this for a minute, as you consider the motives of the diesel generator for telling you this obvious lie.

V

A mere shadow of a man on my dashboard. The child of the diesel generator says, today I feel like a child. I feel that I am falling. A sense of wonder at the smell of wood smoke, the bark of a tree and the bark of a dog, a barked knuckle. The worth of a child is measurable, says the diesel generator, in the context of shadows cast on a wall and the weight of the shadow of a grown man crying, there, on the somber dashboard.

VI

Cabbage, says the diesel generator, and potatoes are the foodstuffs of love, but the memory of a distant hand is like a gingham dress, wet at the hem. This is a false claim, the swell of a hand, a soft girl running her fingers through rich fur. When did we stop talking about food? asks the diesel generator, when a deep rumbling sound marks the presence of something other than rational thought. The worth of the diesel generator can be measured in coins deposited in a glistening slot. Please use exact change only.

VII

Flying to the moon is interesting to the diesel generator, but only after midnight on the night of a full moon. He prefers suitcases that roll, and he prefers rolling them quickly down a tiled hallway so that he may hear the rhythmic clacking of wheels. A wheel symbolizes peace, says the diesel generator, in that it may carry me to the next empty room. A wing symbolizes peace in that it may carry me to the edge of thought, at which appetites dance like girls in the bottom of a drunken boat. The diesel generator is amused by this allusion as he stows his luggage carefully in the overhead compartment so that any shifting during the flight will be minimized, all the while noticing the brightness of the runway in the reflected light of the fullest moon.

VIII

Nothing winged, nothing consisting of hair or teeth or blisters. In the corner of a basement room a tear fell from the ceiling. Sad coupling ensued. It was the end of a long day at the foundry and the heat had taken its toll on the both of you. The diesel generator sat motionless in the dark. It would be days before the story of the killing made sense to anyone. It had been a cold month, to be sure, and the diesel generator had been indispensable. Images of it cluttered the landscape. Several winding paths ended at the base of the diesel generator. Here, even light succumbed to gravity. The rest was history. The rest was a study in trajectories.

IX

Someone is dead, says the diesel generator. Someone is always dead at the end of the day. During the night, too. If you know one man who is dead, you know two men who are dead. Several women, too, are dead. Out on that sidewalk is someone walking who is dead. The dead are singing. The dead are singing the national anthem of the dead in a voice not theirs. The dead are walking in a pair of boots that are not theirs, boots in which they cannot be buried. These words belong to the dead, says the diesel generator, and gives up the words, then lies down carefully to prepare for his own death which will occur momentarily.

X

The diesel generator wants to talk about pain and suffering, the bullet holes in the wall of the hotel, and the great protest in the train station. We had no money, says the diesel generator, and the banks were all closed so we couldn't eat. We slept on baggage carts while all around us, the anger rose like the temperature of a mortally sick child. All this followed idyllic days on the water. Where are those days now? asks the diesel generator, these thirty years distant, and, as if in somber response, a cloud moves slowly toward the sea, off somewhere, out over the horizon.

XI

The diesel generator wears the sweaters of the dead. In light of this, how can memory stain the dolorous walls of the room of the woman in the dream? Surely, the sweaters are warm. Surely, the one small heater is in working condition. Then the diesel generator recalls the scent of latex. The diesel generator recalls the sound of footsteps in the hall, the whoosh of the sliding glass door opening. The diesel generator, surely, maintains a safe distance from such sad memories. He recalls climbing the stairs, standing at the sink, opening the last vision of wanton lust. The door closing, again and again and again. The hand of a woman climbing up his leg. The dead man standing on the balcony. The moon rising over the mountain. The moon rising over the mountain.

Bernd Sauermann

XII

We are not silent. We play the cast iron flutes of the mythic. We are the sound, the source of everything good, says the diesel generator, and the source of everything bad. We leave the conversation there. An agreement has been reached. It is then the diesel generator remembers the fine carpet, the way it soaked up the sounds of water dripping. All water is not tears falling from the eyes of a woman in a basement room, the diesel generator reminds himself. All flutes are not the instruments of nostalgia. All things mythical are not mythical. But by then, the silence, slowly, has been soaked up by the silence.

XIII

The diesel generator can read no further. There on a rainy fall day an epiphany is received like a phone call to say that the items left in the attic have been sold at auction. Sold: a method for penetrating the frozen lake. Sold: the old red couch. Sold: a method for suspension of disbelief at the nature of weather vs. the heat in a room filled with the laughter and the soft touches shaped by the great want. Two people ignite and their flames linger when the diesel generator's remorse is rendered obsolete by the wood stove. The diesel generator carefully folds some feelings and tosses them into the stove, where they catch fire instantly. And so the rhyme is closed, and so the heart is magically removed.

XIV

Tender are the oversized shoes on the sidewalk of sunlit lust. Oh to walk in wanton light on a summer's day down at the reservoir. I have two secrets in the bushes, the diesel generator says, and just down from the hill where the Neanderthals hunted at night. When they were done, he says, they came home to their women and unrolled the fur from their women's legs so tenderly for such brutish creatures. Suddenly the diesel generator feels aware of his own cracked nails and what passes for rational thought in his own reflective head gasket. I have one more secret, thinks the diesel generator, looking wistfully out at the sidewalk.

XV

Ribbons of a dog's howl in the valley, the radio, an old couch in the attic. These are the props of a promised land gone since the seas were first walked upon and the candle was yet to be invented. The diesel generator is heavy and heavily lost in thought. He does not make the sign for victory. This is the sign for an uneasy truce, he says, and holds up the tightly twisted cord in the dimly lit room where the radio stays on all night long playing one foreign language station after another. Then the diesel generator blows out the candle. Somewhere in the darkness, a meetinghouse bell rings.

XVI

I label everything so that I may know that everything has been approved by me, says the diesel generator. I have made a label for my label maker and I have made a label for your love of napping on Sunday afternoons in front of the closed window as a slow rain blurs the sounds of those who walk by. A car sits waiting for service in the parking lot. There is soft rain on its windshield. A girl waits for a window to open. The diesel generator labels this situation with a label reading "Pleasant Situation," then sits back for a smoke labeled "The History of Regret in New England: The Formative Years."

XVII

Satellites move in languid arcs as plans are made and plans are broken. There is a woman in the sleeping house and she sashays and smells of laughter. Come here, says the man, and she does, and the diesel generator nods approvingly as he folds some towels he has just laundered. Your secret is safely locked in my file, thinks the diesel generator as the sky brightens and obscures another satellite transmitting some unheard message through the dark air palpable as a stack of neatly folded laundry.

Bernd Sauermann

XVIII

Offshore, the well of feeling really good, the beachhead of the preserved image and the forgotten paint. The scent of warm water. The shells are tiny here, thinks the diesel generator as he fills up a jar that he will throw out years later, clouded over and altered by persistent misgivings at how he had arranged the people in his life. Sit over here and in this way, commands the diesel generator, as he makes small adjustments based on the angle of his desire. This is the last dead thing I'll ever touch, he thinks, as he etches the image onto what others perceive to be a brilliantly blank canvas.

XIX

Akimbo is an adequate word, thinks the diesel generator as he remembers talk of legs and limbs on the floor of a warm room. The coffee machine gurgled in agreement as plans were made and immediately scrapped in a moment of delight. The death mask had not yet been made and even the man's face had not gone gray and ashen. Once there was a woman in my closet, says the diesel generator, and a light on in the bathroom. It was the funniest thing, he goes on to say, but then the story tapers off into a desperate sobbing that can be heard through a shut closet door.

Bernd Sauermann

XX

The last best thing to happen, the sunny grass, the smell of fresh loam, and the warm wind in my hair was the last thing I felt. This day of memoirs yet to be written, thinks the diesel generator, answers the call of bobcats in the woods, the hooing of owls in the barn on a summer night, the riotous party of the coyotes. Revelry will not end in case of death, the diesel generator says, though it will be more subdued. The sunny grass, yes, and the warm wind in my hair, the wind in my hair and yes, the welcoming smell of freshly turned earth.

XXI

Earth of pinkish delights, the brown curve of a leg in the afternoon of a spring. The flash flood of chemicals in a young brain is easily understood, says the diesel generator, in light of the budding dogwood. The cloudiness of one eye is enough to offset a torrential feeling. Friend, I buried you today in the clear thoughts of the diesel generator as he sat staring at the turn of seasons in an instance of self-reflection unsurprising as a spring rain.

XXII

The loneliness of a sound unheard by the diesel generator, the sum of its parts, and the whole of all passed before me today as I was digging in the garden to plant my heart in the warm earth. To want to straighten that circle was an idea championed by the diesel generator on the day of his conception. There is energy in an unsaid word on a day that will never begin again. There is a day that will never make room for an end, an end that will arrive uninvited by the diesel generator, by the beautiful fact of light and the very force of all that is noticeable only late in the evening.

XXIII

The give and give until you're a cloud and the not blue of a blue sky. The blue not getting bluer and bluer. Then the black. The thing with color, thinks the diesel generator, is that it tells us how to feel, how to put something in the earth on a spring day when the grass solemnly grows toward warmth and a sky that is barely perceived as sunny, a sky which is nothing but blue space between ourselves and a backdrop of grief.

XXIV

Giving up the air beneath the flowers and the rusty nail, the damp stones, the gaze of those to follow. The diesel generator has not spoken before now for a reason. The parts of your feelings, as has been written, are beginning to know a quiet. The peace of the silent, the silence of the before, the before of the after, the duration of all that is no longer. The peace of the diesel generator at rest in the waiting hour.

XXV

Nothing can save me but breasts. The film that plays in the quiet theater, the matinee, the soft seats, the black consuming the white. When can two sides come together in the earth? The diesel generator is not made of steel all the time and can tell the difference between the dark and darkness. He says, I feel in my broken gears that time is receding like a flood. I feel on my worn belts that light is fading like two warm hands, like a pair of soft gloves left out in the snow. Nothing can save me but breasts rising and falling in the silence of projected light and the soft, trembling dark.

XXVI

I want to be trailed by contrails into the past of a color I have yet to feel. That was then and this is the X of the proverbial dotted line. That was then and this is the memory of a face I remember only as being young. The diesel generator feels nostalgic in the dead of night. If only to get there from here, he thinks, if only for the duration of a sigh, the span of time it takes me to recall the exact hue of a closed eye.

XXVII

Pendulum. The good night on the floor of an abandoned house. The phone call late at night. Lava lamp and the soft brush of lips on a shoulder and an epiphany dripping like hot wax. The request for permission and the denial of an answer. The sound of boots in the hall followed by the sound of boots in the hall. The diesel generator, followed by the diesel generator, and then, it goes without saying, the diesel generator.

ACKNOWLEDGEMENTS

Some of the following poems have appeared in *The Round Table, Connotation Press: An Online Artifact, dish, eRatio, Vinyl Poetry, & Anti-*. Horse Less Press published "Diesel Generator" as a chapbook in June 2013.

I would also like to thank the following people for their support, encouragement, criticism, and the occasional dope slap, both physical and metaphysical: Taylor Carlisle, Patrick Condo, Michael Fitzell, Michael Kelsay, Brett Ralph, John Wood, and my family. A special thanks goes to the staff of MadHat Press: Publisher Marc Vincenz, Managing Editor Jonathan Penton, and former Managing Editor Susan Lewis, and Jen Tynes and Michael Sikkema at Horse Less Press.

ABOUT THE AUTHOR

Born in Hof, Germany, **Bernd Sauermann** graduated in 1993 from McNeese State University with an MA in English and an MFA in Creative Writing (poetry). Since then, Sauermann has taught at colleges in Illinois and Vermont and currently teaches composition, literature, creative writing, and film in the Division of Fine Arts and Humanities at Hopkinsville Community College in Hopkinsville, Kentucky.

   Bernd is also an associate editor at *Posit*, an online journal of literature and art, and was the poetry editor at *Whole Beast Rag*, a now-retired online journal of literature, art, and ideas. He's had poems, stories and photographs published in the *McSweeney's Book of Poets Picking Poets, McSweeney's, Southern Indiana Review, New Orleans Review, Nimrod, Poet Lore*, the *Kansas Quarterly Review of Literature, Leveler, e'Ratio, Vinyl Poetry*, and many other publications.